Strategic Planning

B. Vincent

Published by RWG Publishing, 2021.

While every precaution has been taken in the preparation of this book, the publisher assumes no responsibility for errors or omissions, or for damages resulting from the use of the information contained herein.

STRATEGIC PLANNING

First edition. June 10, 2021.

Written by B. Vincent.

Also by B. Vincent

Affiliate Marketing
Affiliate Marketing

Standalone
Affiliate Recruiting
Business Layoffs & Firings
Business and Entrepreneur Guide
Business Remote Workforce
Career Transition
Project Management
Precision Targeting
Professional Development
Strategic Planning

Strategic Planning

Someone once said planning is bringing the future into the present, so that you can do something about it now. And Brian Tracy tells us a clear vision, backed by definite plans, gives you a tremendous feeling of confidence and personal power. Most people would agree that strategic planning is an essential part of any business or organization's success. It makes people proactive rather than reactive. It gives everyone a clear sense of direction. And yet, too often, it's done ineffectively, or even forgotten altogether. There's no telling how much potential economic success has gone unrealized, due to a failure to take planning seriously. So how do we ensure strategic planning remains a part of our organization, how can we best give this crucial aspect of our business the attention it deserves. And how do we make sure we're not only doing it but doing it right. In this course, we're going to teach you how to do exactly that.

95% of a typical workforce doesn't understand its organization's strategy.

90% of organizations fail to implement their strategies, 86% of executive teams spend less than one hour per month discussing strategic planning. These statistics show that strategic planning is an increasingly important area that businesses should focus on.

Our course is going to consist of a series of critical discussion points. These are designed to cover this broad topic as thoroughly as possible, to encourage growth in these vital areas, and to facilitate a real and fruitful discussion within your organization about how you can improve on these essential characteristics, both at work and in your personal lives in general.

Some of these will be pretty lengthy and some will be relatively straightforward and brief, at the very end of this roadmap, comes the most important final step.

Discussion time do not skip this. This is the most important part of this training.

When you finish this course, you need to spend at least an hour or so, going over the questions we supply at the end, as a group. Whoever's the head honcho in the group should designate a facilitator whose responsibility it is, that each question is covered and that everyone, time permitting, is able to have their say. Make sure all contributions are valued, all suggestions considered, and all opinions respected. So, let's move into the first discussion point.

Create a strategy map, strategy mapping formulated by Robert Kaplan and David Norton is a tool used by organizations to describe and communicate strategies. Essentially, a strategy map is a diagram, outlining the company's objectives on a single page. It visually represents the cause-and-effect relationship of each strategic objective. Strategy maps are effective, for people are visual learners by nature. With the help of such illustrations, your employees can have a clear picture for each strategy, rather when done in a written narrative. Strategy maps are created during the initial parts of the strategic planning process, and also used as the main reference material for periodic check-ins and review meetings.

The main idea of a strategic map is that every objective is represented by a shape, usually an oval or rectangle. These objectives are then grouped into categories. However, it's very unlikely for a company to have 20 or more objectives. Having too many objectives to track can mess up the overall message and will only make the strategy difficult to communicate.

Once objectives are established, you then have to sort them into categories, also known as perspectives. Another thing to point out here is that, unlike other diagrams, strategy maps are read from the bottom up, but you build it from the top down.

There are four main perspectives in strategy map. Number one, financial, from the word itself, you should group every financial objective into this category. Basically, any objective relating to the company's financial health and performance should be included in this perspective, revenue, and profit, are the most obvious ones, other objectives may include cost savings and efficiency, adding revenue sources, profit margins. Number two, customer, this perspective focuses on consumers and the market, your objectives should be aligned on how you can deliver better service to the public. These objectives can include improved customer experience, boost market shares, increase brand awareness. Number three, internal processes, this perspective contains processes that help deliver customer and financial objectives. Each should be composed of internal operational goals and then the business needs to drive better performance. Internal processes can include objectives like improve internal efficiency, increase acquisition, increase consulting knowledge, improve product or service offerings.

Number four, learning and growth. While the internal processes focus on the concrete side of processes, this perspective focuses on the intangible aspect of performance drivers. This can include increased expertise, optimize technology, optimize human capital, improve thought leadership. Once you've categorized the objectives to these perspectives you then now have to put arrows, starting from the bottom. These arrows will show the cause-and-effect relationship between each objective. The arrow pads serve as a guide to see how the objectives in the lower perspective contribute to the success of the higher ones.

Strategy maps are used for better communication between employees. When they clearly understand how the objectives relate to one another and how their jobs can contribute to the success of the company. It keeps everyone on the same page, but most importantly, it boosts their morale and productivity.

Make an action plan, strategic planning involves no ad-libbing, you need to create a solid action plan in order for a strategic plan to be successful. Sadly, this step has often been overlooked. Some people are so focused on the outcome, that they forget to plan all the steps needed to achieve that goal.

In fact, some even set goals without even knowing how to achieve them. Here are the components of an action plan, a well-defined description of the goal to be achieved. Outline of tasks that need to be carried out, people who will be in charge of carrying out each task, milestones, deadlines, resources needed to complete each task, and measures to evaluate progress.

Having an action plan provides a clear direction of how you want to achieve each goal. It helps you to stay committed throughout each project. Moreover, action plans encourage you to prioritize tasks based on effort and impact.

Create a vision statement, a vision statement is the company's roadmap, defining the direction of the company's growth. It is the groundwork of your strategic planning for it serves the foundation for a broader strategic plan, compared to general articulations by the management vision statements are formally written and referenced in the company's documents. Here are some key elements of a well-written vision statement. Future-oriented envisions the company's future, not the current. Motivational inspires employees to work harder, they see it as something desirable. Clear and concise, defines a primary goal and is easy to remember. Challenging, something that can't be easily met. Business aligned, should reflect the company's culture and core values. Of course, situations will change, this is why your vision statement should be reviewed periodically. This is to ensure that your objectives are still aligned with the direction you see for the company. A well-written vision statement will direct the company to its full potential. It will serve as a touchstone for your future actions.

Set a mission statement, a mission statement defines the company's purpose and existence. It should identify who your primary customers are, the products or services you offer, and should also describe the geographical location on which you operate. Mission statements and vision statements are often mistaken for one another, for they are correlated. However, the key difference is that mission statements are focused on the present. While the vision is focused on the future. In essence, a mission statement is who we are, while the vision statement is where we are going.

Mission statements are brief into the point, usually composed of one to two sentences. These sentences should clearly define the overall purpose of your company. Here's how to write a mission statement. Step one, what? The first thing you need to do is outline what your company does. This could be a service that you provide or a product that you produce for your customers. In other words, write down whatever makes your company run.

Step two, how? Next, you should describe how your company does what it does. In other words, describe what the company standards are. Think of the core values that go into your business. For instance, maybe you value the quality, the customer satisfaction experience, or maybe you strive to be sustainable and innovative, make sure that these key points are included in the mission statement.

Step three, why? Lastly, you should include the reason why you want to do your mission, briefly explaining your why helps your business stand out and sets you apart from other competitors. After you've made your draft, take the time to review and edit your work or your goals realistic and attainable. Also, make sure to remove all the fancy business jargon. This will only make the mission statement look exaggerated and incomprehensible.

Once you feel that you're satisfied with what you've written, it still doesn't end there. You need to hear the opinions from the other side of the coin, or in other words, you need to gather employee input, select two or three key members of your team, let them review your work, let them know that you value their comments and suggestions and that you're willing to make adjustments if needed. Once you've all agreed, and satisfied with your mission statement, communicate to everyone in the company. Finally, this mission statement should be incorporated into the business website and be an integral part of your ad campaigns.

Conduct a SWOT analysis, a SWOT analysis is a notable strategic technique that helps an organization assess its business. The primary objective of SWOT is to help companies develop a full awareness of their internal and external factors that can affect a business's decision. A SWOT analysis must be done before goal setting, to ensure that the goals you set complement the needs of your company. Here's the breakdown of SWOT, strengths, what are we good at. weaknesses, what areas do we need to improve. Opportunities, what opportunities are in store for us. And threats, what can potentially harm the organization. A SWOT analysis is beneficial for it's a source of information for strategic planning. It recognizes core strengths, reverses the weaknesses, maximizes opportunities, and avoids organizational threats. By reviewing past and current performances, it helps the company to chalk up its plans for the future.

Identify your core values, core values are the beliefs and behaviors of your organization. These are traits that you possess that will enable you to achieve your vision and mission. Core values also serve as a guide, helping your business to stay on the right track. Core values dictate the company's behavior and create a big impact on your business strategy. With well-defined core values, you can build great teams, deliver excellent customer service, and foster innovation. Core values can include the following: trust, integrity, boldness, commitment, accountability, passion, honesty, leadership, innovation, humor, humility, diversity, collaboration, quality, simplicity, ownership, result-oriented, constant improvement. Are you looking for inspiration? Look at how Coca-Cola describes their core values.

Leadership, the courage to shape a better future. Collaboration, leverage collective genius. Integrity, be real. Accountability, if it is to be, It's up to me. Passion committed in heart and mind. Diversity, as inclusive as our brands. And quality, what we do, we do well.

What are the benefits of establishing core values in your business? Number one, it distinguishes a company's identity. A company's identity becomes unique when they reflect what they care about. When you are workers, clients and potential customers understand what the company stands for, it boosts its competitiveness in the marketplace.

Number two improves recruitment and increases retention rate. Employees often want to work with organizations that share the same core values as them. Moreover, when a company religiously adheres with their values, it encourages workers to stay even when things get tough.

Number three helps in decision making. Understanding the core values makes decision-making much easier. For instance, if one of your core values is providing high-quality materials. You don't want to compromise by selling substandard products.

Number four contributes to the overall success of the company. Core values are never compromised. When a company strengthens its resolve in complying with its values, it will surely lead to better outcomes in marketing, human resources, and product innovation.

Build a strategic planning team, as a business owner, you shouldn't feel that you have to do all this by yourself. After all, you already have too much on your plate, having a team that you can collaborate with will make strategic planning much easier for you to manage. This team plays a great role in the success of your strategic plan. Having diverse thoughts and contrasting opinions on organizational matters are keys to creating a solid strategy and building a more productive organization. To build a strong strategy team carefully consider these four points: One, choose the right people. As the strategy team, they are responsible for determining the structure and governance, and path of the company. That being said, the members should be harmoniously aligned with organizational goals. They should also be seen as role models, inspiring other employees to embrace the company's strategy and processes. Two select leaders in every level. Don't assume that leaders only refer to the top executives of the organization. In reality, leaders can be found at any level of your organization.

In fact, there are a lot of mid-level leaders who act beyond the top executives that might go unnoticed and unsung by many. Involving mid-level leaders in strategic planning can help the organization to be aligned with adopted processes and behaviors, having leaders that can relate and reach other workers at every level will surely drive your strategy to success.

Three, have people with diverse viewpoints. If your company has been long governed by the upper echelons of the organization, choosing the same group will not lead to your desired change. Valued viewpoints from all levels are needed to make the needed changes. To do this, you should identify the influencers at every level of the organization. These members serve as change agents that possess lateral thinking. Though it may seem counterintuitive, you should also select leaders that are resistant to change. Having those who are reluctant to revision, gives them an opportunity to yield and embrace the new strategic plan. Four, they possess valuable traits, your team should be humble and receptive to change. They are those who are not content with what's current. Rather, they are those who are yearning for improvement and innovation. These members are transparent and are willing to communicate and debate for the company's greater good.

Lastly, they should be unanimously committed to implementing the strategic plan and willing to embody the necessary changes when needed. The success of your strategic plan relies on the composition and commitment of the team. But assembling this group of people, not only helps you make decisions and things much easier, but they provide a major influence on what lies ahead, of your organization

Established SMART goals. failed strategic planning often comes from poor goal setting. Ill-considered plans are time wasters, that will only lead to marry chasing, to get work done the right way, create goals the right way, work smart using SMART goals. You may have heard this a few times in the previous lessons. The reason being is that this is such an effective way of crafting a goal.

So again, what does a SMART goal mean? Specific, your goals should be well defined vividly describing what you want to achieve. The key to being specific is knowing your why. Understanding your true motives ignite your will to stay on track. The more specific and amplified your goals are, the more likely you'll succeed. Measurable, your goals should be perceptible, or in other words, you can easily track its progress. You make your goals measurable by breaking it down to precise metrics. Measurable goals let you assess your progress, and most importantly, it lets you know when you've achieved it.

However, when creating measurable goals, it's important to leave room for growth. This means that you should consider your limitations and allocate a reasonable time to adjust. Achievable, we all know the saying, dream big, aim high. True, we should set goals that push us beyond our comfort zone. However, we should avoid having lofty goals. Being over-ambitious will only lead you to discouragement, eventually putting your goals down the drain. Achievable goals are initially overwhelming but can really be completed. Relevant, of course, we want our goals to be aligned with our priorities. This means that your greatest dream should always be linked to every goal you're trying to achieve. Every goal should serve as a steppingstone to your ideal vision of success. Time-bound every goal needs a deadline; assign a due date to every goal you make. This pushes you to your limits, positively forcing you to work even harder to reach it. Using smart goals, it helps the company to aim high. It gives you focus, clarity, and motivation that are often lost with poor goal setting. Moreover, it creates a path of coordinate and direction, so you can reach your goals quickly.

Use the PEST analysis, A PEST analysis is a strategy tool used by organizations to identify, analyze, organize, and track macroeconomic factors that can impact a business. PEST stands for political, economic, social, and technological forces. Here are examples of what can be included in each factor: political, government policies, bureaucracy, corruption, foreign trade policy, consumer protection laws, future legislation, tax policy, wars, and conflicts, etc.

Economic, economic trends, growth rates, industry growth, international exchange rates, international trade, labor costs, consumer disposable income, unemployment rates, inflation, interest rates, credit availability, monetary policies, raw material costs, etc.

Social, money, customer service, imports, religion, traditions, health work, leisure, population growth, demographics, immigration, emigration, family size, lifestyle trends, etc. And technology, technological infrastructure, technology legislation, consumer access to technology, competitor technology and development, emerging technologies, automation, research and innovation, intellectual property regulation, technology incentives, etc.

To do a PEST analysis carefully consider the following: Brainstorm, collaborate with your team, and identify what you can put in each area. You can do it together as a group, or break it into smaller units, then merge all the contributions. Group, once you have everyone's input bucket the similar ideas and discard in the duplication

Rate, lead your participants rate the gathered ideas by the level of impact it can have on the organization. Allow them to explain their reasoning and ask them to rate the ideas again to see if there are changes. Share, once you've completed your PEST analysis, share the results to relevant stakeholders, and use the report to monitor the progress. Also always remember to repeat the PEST analysis at regular intervals to stay on top of changes and keep your plans up to date.

What are the benefits of PEST analysis? It helps analyze how your strategy would fit in the extensive environment, encourages strategic thinking. Provides a clear analysis of the external influences that affect the organization. Creates more decisive and knowledgeable decision-making processes. Data can be used for planning, marketing, product development, project management, and research papers.

Set KPIs, a Key Performance Indicator or KPI is a metric value that indicates how effective a company is in achieving its strategy objectives. KPIs help to evaluate the success of reaching their goals. Here's how to create a KPI. Write a clear objective, your KPIs should be integral to the business. It needs to express something strategic about what your business is trying to do, share it with your employees. Communication is paramount, your employees need to understand the goals from your perspective and how their help can contribute to the success of the company. Review them periodically, check in with your KPIs from time to time. This is essential to track your progress and assess the company's development. You can do this on a weekly or monthly basis. Make sure it's actionable, divide KPIs to create short-term and long-term goals.

Modify modified to fit changing needs. Organizations adapt to new practices, modify KPIs to complement new changes. Update objectives when needed, businesses evolve and KPIs should too. Regularly check to see if KPIs are needed to be changed or scrapped immediately KPI metrics increase performance visibility, showing those who are performing well and those who are not. It also directs behavior, encouraging a worker to perform better. When companies utilize KPIs. It unites employees to work towards common goals, it also helps in quicker decision making. Information gleaned from KPIs can also help in developing future strategies for the business.

Develop a communication plan, communication is crucial to the effective implementation of a strategic plan. The reason being is that strategic plans rely on the input and commitment of a wide range of individuals. This group of people should be involved and informed in the process of the earliest stages, up to the production of results. Why is communication important? It creates engagement. The significance of communication is often overlooked during the implementation part of the strategic plan. Of course, the people involved are fully aware of what's happening. But those outside remain clueless about what's been taking place. Effective communication means that all members of the organization are well informed and that they understand the importance of implementing such a plan. It generates broad input, one of the important steps of strategic planning is the SWOT analysis mentioned earlier. This analysis includes input from a wide array of individuals, both from inside and outside of the organization. Gathering feedback from the employees, customers, community members, and other integral constituents, ensures that your strategic plan will have an effective impact on the organization.

It helps to test assumptions, the strategy team planning independently may sometimes make assumptions that conflict with the reality in the front lines. This is why communication with your employees is essential, to determine if the right elements are included and that if the goals are clearly aligned with the company's objectives. It provides updates on progress. A lot of times companies failed to execute their strategic plans, because of the lack of updates on the progress. Keep the plan alive by having continuous communication with your employees and share any updates of the progress. Also, make sure that the ones responsible for achieving objectives should give out progress reports regularly.

In order to create an effective communication plan, you should do the following: Present in various ways. Instead of just explaining long-drawn-out information, add creativity to your presentation by using a combination of video, audio, visual, and written formats. Make it clear and relevant, don't assume that your employees know what you're talking about, define your terms and avoid jargon-laden phrases. Instead, use clear and comprehensible language. Develop, bottom-up communication, you need feedback from all levels of your organization. Make sure to develop an avenue for getting constructive feedback from all your employees.

Have regular strategy meetings, from the word itself, these meetings are focused solely on strategy. These are regularly scheduled sessions that use data and track the current progress of the company. Typical review meetings allow you to stop and look at the current data, but strategy meetings take things a step further, allowing you to analyze the data and make needed adjustments. Here are some tips when conducting strategy meetings. Take things critically, people often want to start things with a positive note, if there are negative points that need to be discussed. It shouldn't be included and can even be the focus of the meeting. Respect your participants' time, keep meetings to an appropriate length, avoid having lengthy protracted discussions. Avoid distractions, don't let anyone or anything divert the meeting agenda. A lot of time for private conversations. These are discussions that need to be addressed, but not appropriate for the current meeting. Adhere to the agenda at all times, if possible. If you have to make adjustments, try to adjust for a future meeting, but not the current one. This trains your employees to change their behavior and use their time effectively.

Encourage participation, encourage people to speak up, let them know that their comments are highly valued and needed in every meeting. Your goal is for strategy review meetings to become a norm for the business, make this regular review process sustainable and that people are looking forward to it. Work on continually improving and simplifying processes to make it much easier to handle.

Establish long-term goals, long term goals are targets intended for the future. This requires an extensive amount of time and careful planning. These usually range between three to five years and can even get up to 10 years to achieve. As entrepreneurs, your long-term goals should reflect not only for the growth of the business but your personal interests as well. Here are some practical examples of long-term goals that you can set. Increase sales, expand to new opportunities, increase brand recognition, create a lasting legacy or reputation. Host promotional events, long term goals give you a clear direction of where your business is heading. It gives the team a sense of purpose of having something great to look forward to. Moreover, it helps us to see the bigger picture of what's in store for the organization. Achieving long-term goals creates a long-lasting impact, that contributes to the upward trend of success.

And now, it's discussion time. The most important part of this training, whoever's the head honcho in the group should designate a facilitator whose responsibility it is that each of the questions you see on your screen is covered and that everyone, time permitting, is able to have their say. Make sure all contributions are valued, all suggestions considered, and all opinions respected.

Don't miss out!

Visit the website below and you can sign up to receive emails whenever B. Vincent publishes a new book. There's no charge and no obligation.

https://books2read.com/r/B-A-QWUO-FKLPB

BOOKS 2 READ

Connecting independent readers to independent writers.

Also by B. Vincent

Affiliate Marketing
Affiliate Marketing

Standalone
Affiliate Recruiting
Business Layoffs & Firings
Business and Entrepreneur Guide
Business Remote Workforce
Career Transition
Project Management
Precision Targeting
Professional Development
Strategic Planning

About the Publisher

Accepting manuscripts in the most categories. We love to help people get their words available to the world.

Revival Waves of Glory focus is to provide more options to be published. We do traditional paperbacks, hardcovers, audio books and ebooks all over the world. A traditional royalty-based publisher that offers self-publishing options, Revival Waves provides a very author friendly and transparent publishing process, with President Bill Vincent involved in the full process of your book. Send us your manuscript and we will contact you as soon as possible.

Contact: Bill Vincent at rwgpublishing@yahoo.com www.rwgpublishing.com